MW01593048

Kash Patel

Kash Patel's Plan to Overhaul the FBI, Expose Corruption, and Restore Trust in Law Enforcement

Fred Chandler

Table of Contents

Introduction

A New Era of Leadership

Kash Patel is not just a name in the world of politics and governance—he is a movement, a visionary leader set to redefine how America approaches justice and national security. Born to immigrant parents and raised with a deep sense of patriotism, Patel's journey from an apolitical youth to a national figure represents the transformative power of vision, persistence, and belief in the principles of democracy.

Patel's nomination to lead the FBI under President-elect Donald Trump symbolizes a pivotal shift in American leadership. It reflects the growing demand for innovative, unorthodox approaches to governance. In Patel, many see a leader unafraid to challenge entrenched systems, question long-held traditions, and dismantle bureaucracies that have, in his words, prioritized political bias over justice. His rise signals not only a generational change but also the emergence of leadership that embraces transparency, accountability, and the restoration of public trust.

Patel's leadership philosophy is rooted in the belief that the American justice system must serve all citizens equally, regardless of political affiliation, social status, or ideological leanings. His bold proposals, from decentralizing the FBI to restructuring its leadership, highlight his commitment to breaking down systems he believes have fostered inefficiency and corruption. Kash Patel's era of leadership is one that promises to prioritize the core values of justice: fairness, integrity, and the unwavering pursuit of truth.

Kash Patel's Vision for American Justice

At the heart of Kash Patel's vision is a fundamental question: What does justice truly mean in America today? Patel argues that justice cannot thrive in a system plagued by partisanship, secrecy, and unaccountability. For him, reforming the justice system starts with addressing these systemic issues and creating institutions that uphold the principles of democracy.

One of Patel's most ambitious goals is the overhaul of the FBI, a cornerstone of federal law enforcement. Patel has consistently argued that the agency has grown too large, too centralized, and too detached from its original mission. He envisions a decentralized FBI, with a reduced footprint in Washington, D.C., and more resources allocated to field offices across the nation. This approach, he contends, will bring the agency closer to the communities it serves and foster greater trust between federal law enforcement and the American people.

Patel also seeks to confront what he describes as the "deep state," a network of unelected bureaucrats, media figures, and corporate entities he believes have wielded undue influence over American politics. In his 2023 book, *Government Gangsters*, Patel outlines a blueprint for dismantling this so-called deep state. His vision includes rooting out corruption within federal agencies, holding officials accountable for misconduct, and ensuring that justice is applied equally to all, regardless of political affiliation.

Central to Patel's vision is the principle of accountability. He believes that institutions like the Department of Justice (DOJ) and the FBI must not only be transparent in their operations but also held accountable for their actions. This includes scrutinizing high-ranking officials who, in his view, have used their positions to shield allies and target opponents. Patel's proposals for reform reflect a commitment to creating a justice system that is free from bias and dedicated to upholding the rule of law.

Moreover, Patel's vision extends beyond institutional reform. He emphasizes the need for cultural change within the justice system. He advocates for a shift in mindset, where public servants prioritize service over self-interest and work towards the common good. Patel's leadership style, characterized by his directness, passion, and relentless pursuit of justice, serves as a model for this cultural transformation.

In articulating his vision, Patel often speaks about the importance of restoring faith in the justice system. He acknowledges that many Americans have lost trust in institutions that were once seen as pillars of democracy. Through his reforms, Patel aims to rebuild this trust, ensuring that every citizen feels confident in the fairness and integrity of the justice system.

Kash Patel's vision for American justice is ambitious, unapologetic, and deeply rooted in his belief in the power of the people. As he steps into a role that has the potential to reshape the nation's justice system, Patel brings with him a promise of change—a promise to challenge the status quo, address systemic flaws, and build a system that truly embodies the principles of democracy and equality.

This is the foundation of Kash Patel's story: a leader determined to redefine what it means to serve justice in America. His journey, his philosophy, and his bold vision for the future set the stage for a new chapter in American leadership, one where integrity, accountability, and the pursuit of truth take center stage.

Chapter 1: The Rise of Kash Patel

From Public Defender to National Security Visionary

Kash Patel's ascent to the national stage is nothing short of extraordinary. A first-generation American of Indian heritage, Patel grew up in Queens, New York, in a household that valued education, hard work, and community service. These principles shaped his path as he transitioned from a public defender, tirelessly advocating for the marginalized, to a national security expert with an unwavering commitment to reforming the nation's justice and security apparatus.

Patel's career began in the legal world, where he worked as a public defender in Miami. This role placed him on the front lines of the justice system, defending individuals who often lacked the resources or knowledge to navigate complex legal processes. Patel saw firsthand how socioeconomic disparities and systemic inefficiencies could tilt the scales of justice. These early experiences instilled in him a belief that the justice system should not only be fair but also accessible and accountable to all Americans.

Patel's success as a public defender was marked by his ability to blend legal acumen with compassion. He didn't merely see his clients as case numbers; he saw them as people whose stories mattered. This commitment to serving the underrepresented solidified his reputation as a dedicated and effective advocate. It also laid the groundwork for his later efforts to reform larger institutions, where he would bring the same passion for justice and equity.

Recognizing the need to address systemic issues beyond individual cases, Patel transitioned to a career in national security. His move to Washington, D.C., was driven by a desire to serve his country on a broader scale. Patel joined the Department of Justice (DOJ), where he worked on counterterrorism cases and national security issues. His time at the DOJ was transformative, exposing him to the intricacies of federal law enforcement and the challenges of balancing security with civil liberties.

Patel's expertise and dedication caught the attention of key figures in government, leading to his role as a senior advisor in various capacities, including at the National Security Council (NSC). At the NSC, he became a trusted voice on matters of counterterrorism and intelligence. Patel played a pivotal role in crafting strategies to address emerging threats, from foreign adversaries to domestic security challenges. His ability to navigate complex geopolitical landscapes and his commitment to transparency set him apart as a visionary leader in national security.

Perhaps one of Patel's most notable contributions during this period was his work on exposing abuses of power within the intelligence community. He gained national recognition for his role as lead investigator in the House Intelligence Committee's inquiry into the FBI's handling of the Russia investigation. Patel's findings highlighted what he described as systemic flaws and political bias within the nation's top intelligence agencies. His work not only cemented his reputation as a reformer but also underscored his belief in the need for accountability at the highest levels of government.

Patel's journey from public defender to national security visionary demonstrates his unique ability to adapt and excel in vastly different roles. Whether advocating for clients in a courtroom or addressing global security challenges, Patel has consistently demonstrated a commitment to justice, fairness, and the rule of law. His diverse experiences have shaped his holistic approach to leadership, one that prioritizes both individual rights and national interests.

Kash's Early Life and Inspirational Beginnings

Kash Patel's story begins in a modest household in Queens, New York, where he was raised by immigrant parents who instilled in him a strong sense of duty and resilience. His parents, who came to America in search of better opportunities, emphasized the importance of education and hard work as the keys to success. These values became the foundation of Patel's character, guiding him through every stage of his career.

Patel's upbringing was marked by the challenges and triumphs typical of immigrant families. He grew up in a multicultural environment, surrounded by people from diverse backgrounds. This exposure to different cultures and perspectives helped shape his worldview, fostering a deep appreciation for the principles of democracy and equality that define America.

As a young boy, Patel showed an early interest in public service. He often spoke of wanting to make a difference in the world, a dream inspired by his parents' sacrifices and the opportunities they had created for him. This aspiration led him to pursue higher education, first at the University of Richmond, where he studied government and international relations, and later at Pace University's School of Law.

During his time in law school, Patel's focus on justice and advocacy became clear. He excelled academically while also participating in internships and programs that allowed him to engage directly with the legal system. Patel's experiences during these formative years reinforced his belief that the law could be a powerful tool for promoting fairness and equality.

Patel's early life is a testament to the power of perseverance and purpose. Despite facing obstacles, he remained steadfast in his commitment to serving others. His journey from a humble upbringing to a prominent role in national security reflects not only his personal determination but also the opportunities that America offers to those willing to work hard and dream big.

Today, Patel often credits his parents and his early experiences for shaping his approach to leadership. He speaks passionately about the importance of remembering one's roots and using one's platform to give back to the community. For Patel, leadership is not about personal ambition; it is about making a meaningful impact and ensuring that future generations have the same opportunities he did.

Kash Patel's rise is more than a personal success story; it is an inspiring example of how dedication, vision, and an unwavering belief in justice can lead to transformative change. From his humble beginnings to his role as a national security expert, Patel embodies the values of hard work, integrity, and service that define true leadership. This chapter sets the stage for understanding the man behind the mission and the principles that drive his ambitious vision for America's future.

Chapter 2: A Patriot's Foundation

Core Beliefs and America First Values

Kash Patel's vision for America is grounded in a deep respect for the nation's founding principles, along with a commitment to the values that he believes have made America an exceptional force on the global stage. Patel's core beliefs are shaped by his personal experiences, his legal and security background, and a profound understanding of the challenges and opportunities that lie ahead for the country. As a dedicated patriot, Patel's commitment to America first values has been central to his professional endeavors, guiding his policy decisions and national security strategies.

At the heart of Patel's worldview is the belief in American sovereignty, freedom, and the rule of law. He is a firm advocate for policies that prioritize the nation's security and economic prosperity, while ensuring that the American people's freedoms are protected from both foreign and domestic threats. This commitment to safeguarding America's interests, both at home and abroad, is what Patel believes distinguishes America as a leader among nations.

For Patel, the concept of "America First" is not just a slogan; it is a guiding philosophy that influences everything from foreign policy to domestic economic decisions. It is about ensuring that the interests of the American people come before any external pressures, whether from global organizations or foreign governments. This mindset drives his stance on issues such as immigration reform, trade policies, and military engagements. Patel sees America as a beacon of hope and liberty, and believes that the nation should not only defend its values but also promote them on the global stage.

One of Patel's central beliefs is that America's national security must be prioritized above all else. As a national security expert, he understands that the safety of the American people and the integrity of the nation's borders are paramount to the country's future. He is an advocate for strengthening the military, improving intelligence capabilities, and ensuring that law enforcement agencies have the resources they need to protect the American public. This approach, according to Patel, is not only vital for America's defense but also critical for maintaining global stability in an increasingly volatile world.

Patel's view of the world is one that sees America as a force for good. He is committed to ensuring that the nation's foreign policy is rooted in strength, respect for allies, and a clear-eyed approach to adversaries. Under Patel's leadership, America would be prepared to defend its interests and those of its allies, while also fostering economic growth and technological innovation. Patel believes that a strong America is an essential component of global peace and prosperity, and that the country must be unapologetic in its pursuit of these goals.

Central to Patel's philosophy is a belief in accountability and transparency. Throughout his career, he has worked to expose corruption and inefficiencies within the government and the intelligence community. Patel views these efforts as part of his broader mission to create a government that is accountable to the people, and one that serves their interests first and foremost. He advocates for reducing the size of the federal government and ensuring that it operates with the highest levels of integrity and efficiency.

Patel's America First values also extend to economic policies. He is a strong proponent of free-market capitalism and believes that economic growth should be driven by private enterprise, not government intervention. He supports policies that foster innovation, reduce regulations, and lower taxes, all of which he sees as key to unlocking America's economic potential. In Patel's vision, a thriving economy is one that benefits all Americans, creating opportunities for hard-working individuals and families to succeed.

Furthermore, Patel is a staunch defender of American exceptionalism. He believes that America's unique political and cultural foundation has allowed it to become a beacon of hope and opportunity for people around the world. The ideals of liberty, individual rights, and self-determination are what set America apart from other nations, and Patel is dedicated to ensuring that these principles continue to define the country's future. For him, America's greatness lies in its unwavering commitment to these core values.

The Influence of Immigrant Upbringing

Kash Patel's immigrant upbringing has had a profound impact on his worldview, shaping both his core beliefs and his approach to leadership. As the son of Indian immigrants who came to the United States in pursuit of a better life, Patel's experiences growing up in a diverse, working-class neighborhood in Queens, New York, helped mold his perspective on what it means to be an American and how America should approach both domestic and foreign policy.

Patel often speaks about the sacrifices his parents made to give him the opportunities that would allow him to succeed. His father, a small-business owner, and his mother, a teacher, both instilled in him a deep respect for the value of hard work and perseverance. They emphasized the importance of taking responsibility for one's actions and striving for excellence in all areas of life. These values have been central to Patel's approach to both his career and his vision for the future of the United States.

The immigrant experience has also influenced Patel's understanding of American exceptionalism. Growing up in an immigrant household, he saw firsthand the opportunities that the United States provides to those who are willing to work hard and pursue their dreams. This unique perspective has shaped Patel's commitment to preserving the American Dream and ensuring that future generations have the same opportunities that he was afforded. For Patel, America's success is rooted in its ability to welcome immigrants and offer them a chance to build a better life while adhering to the country's core principles of freedom, equality, and justice.

Patel's immigrant upbringing has also influenced his views on immigration policy. He understands the importance of securing America's borders and ensuring that immigration is managed in a way that prioritizes the safety and interests of American citizens. At the same time, Patel is committed to maintaining the country's reputation as a land of opportunity. He supports policies that provide a pathway to citizenship for law-abiding immigrants, particularly those who contribute to the nation's economy and cultural diversity. For Patel, immigration reform is about finding a balance between securing the country's borders and continuing to uphold the values that make America a beacon for those seeking a better life.

Ultimately, Patel's immigrant background has played a crucial role in shaping his vision for America. It has instilled in him a deep appreciation for the opportunities that the country provides, as well as a sense of duty to protect and strengthen the nation for future generations. His upbringing has made him acutely aware of the importance of preserving America's identity and ensuring that the country remains a place where hard work, dedication, and perseverance are rewarded.

Kash Patel's patriotism and his America First values are not only a reflection of his personal experiences but also a testament to the power of the American experiment. His immigrant roots have shaped his belief in the potential of every individual to succeed, and this belief underpins his vision for the future of the country. For Patel, being an American is not just about living in a particular place; it is about embracing the principles of freedom, opportunity, and responsibility that define the nation's identity.

Chapter 3: Reforming the FBI – A Blueprint for Change

The Call for a Decentralized FBI

Throughout his career, Kash Patel has been a staunch advocate for reforming institutions that he believes have become entrenched in inefficiency, political bias, and a failure to serve the American people. Among these institutions, the FBI has long been a focal point of his criticism. In Patel's view, the FBI has drifted away from its core mission of upholding the rule of law and protecting national security, becoming a tool for political agendas rather than an impartial force for justice.

Patel believes that the FBI, in its current form, has grown too centralized and too powerful, leading to a lack of accountability and transparency. The centralized structure of the FBI, with its decision-making concentrated at the top, creates a disconnect between the agency and the American public. Patel argues that this centralization of power has contributed to the agency's politicization, where decisions about investigations and actions are often influenced by political considerations rather than the pursuit of justice.

The solution, according to Patel, lies in decentralizing the FBI's structure. He envisions a system where local field offices have more autonomy to make decisions based on the needs and concerns of their communities, rather than being subject to top-down directives from Washington, D.C. By decentralizing the FBI, Patel believes the agency can better serve its primary mission of protecting national security and enforcing the law without the distractions of political influence.

A decentralized FBI, in Patel's vision, would involve greater accountability at the local level, where agents and officials are more in tune with the issues facing their respective regions. This approach would allow for quicker, more efficient responses to threats, as decisions would be made closer to the ground where the intelligence is being gathered. The decentralization of power would also ensure that local FBI offices have the flexibility to prioritize their efforts in accordance with the specific needs of their communities, rather than being dictated by a distant headquarters.

Patel's proposed reform would also include an overhaul of the FBI's leadership structure. He advocates for leadership that is more transparent, accountable, and less prone to political influence. In his view, the FBI should be led by individuals who have a deep commitment to the agency's mission and a clear understanding of the challenges posed by modern threats, including terrorism, cybercrime, and domestic extremism. By restructuring the FBI's leadership, Patel believes the agency could once again become the impartial institution it was originally designed to be, free from the political pressures that have clouded its actions in recent years.

Additionally, Patel's decentralization plan would focus on restoring the agency's role as a neutral force for justice. Under his vision, the FBI would prioritize its core functions—national security, counterintelligence, and law enforcement—without being diverted by partisan agendas. He argues that such a shift in focus would restore the public's trust in the FBI, ensuring that it is seen as a defender of the law rather than a political tool.

In summary, Kash Patel's call for a decentralized FBI is rooted in a desire to restore integrity and accountability to the agency. By empowering local offices, increasing transparency, and removing political influence from decision-making processes, Patel believes the FBI can be reformed into an agency that is more effective, efficient, and responsive to the needs of the American people.

Turning the FBI Headquarters into a Museum of the Deep State

One of the more controversial aspects of Kash Patel's vision for reforming the FBI is his bold suggestion to turn the FBI Headquarters in Washington, D.C., into a "Museum of the Deep State." This proposal reflects Patel's deeply held belief that the FBI, as it currently operates, has become a symbol of the "Deep State"—a term used to describe a shadowy network of bureaucrats, intelligence officials, and political operatives who, in Patel's view, wield excessive influence over American policy and decision-making.

For Patel, the FBI headquarters has become a symbol of the corruption and politicization that he believes has infected the agency. He argues that the agency has drifted far from its original mandate of protecting national security and enforcing the law, and instead has become a political actor in its own right. Patel contends that this has been most evident in the FBI's involvement in high-profile political investigations, such as the Russia collusion probe and the investigation into the Clinton email scandal, where he believes the agency demonstrated clear bias and partisanship.

In Patel's vision, transforming the FBI Headquarters into a museum would serve as a powerful statement about the need to reform not just the agency itself but the broader systems of government that have allowed such corruption to flourish. The museum would serve as a place for the American public to learn about the FBI's history, its successes, and its failures—particularly the instances in which the agency overstepped its bounds and became entangled in political controversies. By turning the headquarters into a museum, Patel suggests, the FBI's troubled history could be documented and examined, while also signaling a commitment to transparency and accountability moving forward.

This proposal is particularly focused on what Patel describes as the "Deep State" elements within the FBI—the entrenched bureaucrats and officials who, he believes, work behind the scenes to push their own agendas, regardless of the political party in power. For Patel, the Deep State is a major obstacle to the effective functioning of American government, as it represents a concentration of power in the hands of unelected individuals who operate outside the public's view and beyond the reach of democratic accountability. The Museum of the Deep State would, in Patel's eyes, symbolize the need to dismantle these power structures and restore the FBI to its original mission.

Patel's suggestion to transform the FBI Headquarters into a museum is, of course, a highly provocative and controversial one. Critics argue that such a move would be an affront to the agency's history and a disservice to the many dedicated professionals within the FBI who have served honorably throughout its existence. However, for Patel, the museum is not intended as a disrespectful gesture but as a powerful symbol of accountability, a reminder that even the most powerful institutions must be held to account when they deviate from their fundamental purpose.

This idea also aligns with Patel's broader vision of government reform. He believes that the FBI, like many other federal agencies, has grown too powerful and too unaccountable, and that steps must be taken to restore the balance of power between the government and the people. By creating a museum, Patel hopes to highlight the need for structural changes within the FBI and other government agencies, ensuring that they remain true to their original purpose and are no longer susceptible to the whims of the political class.

Ultimately, Patel's suggestion to turn the FBI Headquarters into a Museum of the Deep State is emblematic of his broader approach to government reform: a willingness to challenge the status quo, confront entrenched bureaucracies, and push for a more accountable and transparent government. While controversial, the proposal underscores Patel's commitment to addressing the systemic issues that he believes have allowed the Deep State to flourish within the FBI and other key institutions. In his vision, such reforms are necessary to restore public trust in government and to ensure that the American people are served by institutions that are truly working for their benefit.

Chapter 4: The Deep State Exposed

Breaking Down the Concept of the Deep State

The term "Deep State" has gained widespread attention in recent years, often used to describe a shadowy network of powerful bureaucrats, intelligence officials, and political elites who operate outside of the public eye, wielding substantial influence over government policy and decision-making. Kash Patel has been one of the most vocal proponents of the notion that the Deep State exists within the American government, particularly within agencies like the FBI, CIA, and the Department of Justice. To Patel, the Deep State represents a corrupt and unaccountable faction of the government that works in secret to push its own agenda, often to the detriment of the American people and the democratic process.

At its core, Patel's conception of the Deep State revolves around the idea that a select group of unelected officials hold disproportionate power and influence over the direction of the country. These individuals, in Patel's view, often work behind the scenes to advance their own political or ideological goals, disregarding the will of the people or the duly elected leadership of the country. The Deep State, Patel argues, is characterized by a lack of transparency and accountability, operating in a way that makes it difficult for the public to fully understand or scrutinize its actions.

Patel's experience as a former senior official in the Trump administration has shaped his views on the Deep State. Throughout his tenure, Patel saw what he considered to be numerous instances of government agencies, particularly the FBI and CIA, engaging in what he views as politically motivated actions. For example, he points to the FBI's handling of the investigation into Hillary Clinton's email server and the Russia collusion investigation, arguing that these were emblematic of the agency's politicization. Patel believes that these actions were the result of individuals within the FBI and other agencies who were more concerned with advancing a particular political agenda than with serving the public or following the law.

The Deep State, according to Patel, is not a monolithic entity but rather a loose collection of individuals and factions embedded within various government agencies, the media, and even some sectors of the business world. These individuals, Patel argues, often form networks and alliances that transcend political parties and administrations, allowing them to exert their influence over long periods of time. In Patel's view, the Deep State operates by manipulating information, controlling narratives, and using its position of power to push policies that benefit its own interests, rather than those of the American people.

One of the hallmarks of the Deep State, as Patel sees it, is the existence of "leaks" within government agencies—unauthorized disclosures of classified or sensitive information intended to shape public opinion or undermine political leaders who are seen as a threat to the status quo. Patel contends that such leaks are often orchestrated by Deep State actors who wish to influence political outcomes or protect their own interests. This is particularly concerning for Patel, as he believes that these leaks are an abuse of power and undermine the principles of transparency and accountability that are supposed to guide government operations.

In essence, Patel's definition of the Deep State is not limited to a few bad actors but extends to a broader system of entrenched interests that work in secret to manipulate the levers of government power. It is, in Patel's view, a direct threat to democracy, as it allows unelected individuals to hold sway over policy decisions without the oversight or accountability that elected officials are subject to.

Strategies to Restore Transparency and Accountability

If the Deep State represents the unaccountable forces within government that undermine the will of the people, then Patel's mission is to expose these forces and dismantle their power. His approach to combating the Deep State involves several key strategies, all centered on restoring transparency, accountability, and a return to government that is truly of the people, by the people, and for the people.

1. Strengthening Congressional Oversight

Patel is a firm believer in the importance of a robust system of checks and balances in government. One of the primary ways he advocates for restoring transparency and accountability is by strengthening the oversight power of Congress. In Patel's view, Congress has been far too passive in holding agencies like the FBI and CIA accountable for their actions. He argues that the legislative branch must use its investigative powers to ensure that agencies are acting in accordance with the law and are not using their power for political purposes.

Patel's proposed reforms include expanding Congressional oversight committees, increasing the frequency and depth of agency audits, and requiring government agencies to testify before Congress more regularly. This, he believes, would create a system of accountability where government agencies would be forced to justify their actions and demonstrate that they are operating transparently and in the best interests of the American people. Patel has pointed to his own experiences working with Congressional committees as evidence of how effective such oversight can be in exposing government overreach and wrongdoing.

2. Dismantling the Bureaucratic Elite

One of the core tenets of Patel's vision for reform is dismantling the entrenched bureaucratic elite that he believes constitutes the Deep State. He argues that many of the individuals who occupy key positions within government agencies are not accountable to the public and often operate in ways that are insulated from scrutiny. Patel's strategy for dealing with this issue involves reducing the power of career bureaucrats and increasing the influence of elected officials in shaping policy decisions.

Patel believes that a major part of this process involves clearing out individuals who have been in their positions for too long and who have become entrenched in the system. This, he argues, is critical for ensuring that government agencies can be reformed and that their leadership is more responsive to the public's needs. He also advocates for introducing term limits for certain high-level bureaucratic positions, ensuring that leadership remains dynamic and accountable to the people.

3. Implementing Transparency in Intelligence and Law Enforcement Operations

A key element of Patel's reform agenda is increasing transparency within the intelligence and law enforcement communities. He believes that many of the Deep State's most egregious actions occur behind closed doors, with little public awareness or oversight. To combat this, Patel calls for greater transparency in how intelligence is gathered, analyzed, and acted upon. This would include regular declassification of intelligence reports, a re-evaluation of the use of classified information, and the creation of mechanisms for the public to have more insight into how decisions are made within these agencies.

Patel also advocates for reforms in law enforcement operations, particularly when it comes to the use of surveillance and investigation techniques. He believes that these tools must be used responsibly and only when there is a clear and justified need. By implementing greater transparency, Patel hopes to ensure that the public can have confidence that government agencies are operating within the bounds of the Constitution and are not engaging in unconstitutional surveillance or other violations of privacy.

4. Building a Culture of Accountability

Ultimately, Patel believes that the most important step in fighting the Deep State is to restore a culture of accountability within the federal government. He argues that this cannot be achieved through top-down reforms alone but must be embedded in the very ethos of how government agencies operate. This means fostering an environment where employees at all levels of government are held to high ethical standards, where whistleblowers are protected, and where those who engage in misconduct are held accountable.

Patel's vision for accountability extends beyond just the FBI and CIA. He calls for similar reforms across all government agencies, including the Department of Justice, the Department of Homeland Security, and the Department of State. By building a culture of accountability, Patel believes that the government can begin to shift away from the entrenched power structures that have allowed the Deep State to thrive, restoring the trust and confidence of the American people.

In conclusion, Kash Patel's strategy for exposing the Deep State and restoring transparency and accountability in government is multi-faceted. It combines strengthening Congressional oversight, dismantling the bureaucratic elite, implementing transparency in intelligence and law enforcement, and building a culture of accountability. Together, these strategies represent Patel's vision for a more open and responsive government—one that serves the interests of the people and is not beholden to the secretive and unaccountable forces that have long manipulated the system for their own gain.

Chapter 5: Leadership Philosophy in Action

Building a New Team of American Patriots

At the core of Kash Patel's leadership philosophy is the belief that effective governance requires strong, principled individuals who are committed to the ideals of justice, transparency, and accountability. Patel's vision for leadership goes beyond traditional political paradigms; it's about creating a new wave of leadership in America—one driven by a deep sense of patriotism, a commitment to serving the public, and an unwavering dedication to restoring the integrity of the nation's institutions.

Patel envisions assembling a team of "American Patriots"—individuals who are not only deeply knowledgeable and skilled but who are also driven by a deep sense of duty to their country. For Patel, a true American patriot is someone who understands the significance of protecting the Constitution, upholding the rule of law, and ensuring that the American people are always at the center of policy decisions. This new generation of leadership, according to Patel, would reject the partisan divides that have plagued the political landscape for years and instead focus on what's best for the country as a whole.

Patel believes that effective leadership requires a shared vision among those in power—a vision grounded in core values like integrity, loyalty to the American people, and a commitment to excellence. This vision is not just about rhetoric or political maneuvering; it's about creating a movement within the government that prioritizes the needs of the people over the desires of special interests, bureaucrats, and entrenched political elites. Patel's approach to building this team starts with recruiting individuals who are not only ideologically aligned but also possess the necessary skills and moral character to tackle the enormous challenges the country faces.

Patel often speaks about the importance of a leadership style that is not top-down but rather one that encourages collaboration, communication, and shared responsibility. He stresses that the team he envisions would be one in which every member is empowered to make decisions and contribute ideas, fostering a sense of ownership and accountability. This approach would create a more dynamic and effective government, where individuals are encouraged to think outside the box, challenge the status quo, and bring innovative solutions to the table.

In Patel's view, the process of building a new team of American patriots involves identifying individuals who are willing to take risks in order to restore the nation's institutions. He believes that the current system of government is not functioning as it should because it has become mired in corruption, bureaucracy, and political infighting. A new team of patriots, Patel argues, is necessary to push back against these forces and re-establish a government that works for the people.

To achieve this, Patel advocates for selecting individuals who have a proven track record of integrity and service, individuals who have demonstrated their commitment to the values that America was built upon. This could mean selecting individuals from outside traditional political circles—people who have proven their ability to lead in other areas, whether in law, business, or military service. Patel emphasizes that patriotism isn't about political affiliation; it's about putting the country first and working together to achieve common goals.

Eliminating Bureaucratic Corruption

A central element of Patel's leadership philosophy is his commitment to eliminating bureaucratic corruption, which he views as one of the greatest obstacles to effective governance. To Patel, bureaucratic corruption is not just about a few bad apples—it's an endemic problem that affects many government agencies, including the FBI, CIA, and the Department of Justice. He argues that these agencies have become too powerful and too insulated from oversight, allowing corruption to take root and flourish.

Patel's solution to this issue is rooted in his belief in the necessity of accountability and transparency. Bureaucratic corruption, in his view, occurs when government officials and agencies operate without the oversight necessary to ensure they are acting in the best interests of the public. This corruption can take many forms, from unethical practices like leaking classified information for political purposes to more systemic issues, such as agencies prioritizing their own power over the needs of the people they are supposed to serve.

For Patel, the first step in eliminating bureaucratic corruption is to change the culture within government agencies. He stresses that leadership must set the tone for the entire organization, and that means rooting out corruption wherever it exists. Patel has long advocated for placing individuals in positions of power who are committed to accountability and transparency, and who will hold others within their agencies to the same standard. He believes that leadership must lead by example and make it clear that unethical behavior will not be tolerated, regardless of rank or political affiliation.

One of Patel's key strategies for eliminating corruption within the bureaucracy is to reduce the power of entrenched bureaucrats who, over time, have become insulated from accountability. Many of these bureaucrats, Patel argues, have been in their positions for so long that they no longer feel any obligation to serve the public or follow the law. By instituting term limits and ensuring that high-level positions are filled with fresh perspectives, Patel believes that it is possible to break the cycle of corruption that has taken hold in many government agencies.

Furthermore, Patel advocates for reforms that would make it easier to fire or remove corrupt officials. Under the current system, it is often difficult to hold bureaucrats accountable for their actions due to the complex legal and procedural barriers in place. Patel has called for reforms to streamline this process, allowing for quicker action against those who violate the public's trust. He also emphasizes the importance of ensuring that whistleblowers—individuals who expose corruption and wrongdoing within government—are protected from retaliation, arguing that these individuals play a critical role in maintaining transparency and accountability within government institutions.

Another element of Patel's approach to eliminating bureaucratic corruption is the need for greater oversight and transparency in the decision-making processes of government agencies. Patel has repeatedly pointed out that one of the key ways to fight corruption is to ensure that government actions are subject to scrutiny, both from other branches of government and from the public. To achieve this, Patel has advocated for more robust Congressional oversight of key agencies, particularly the FBI and CIA, to ensure that they are not operating in secret or outside of the law.

Patel also stresses the need for reforming the hiring and promotion practices within government agencies. He argues that the current system often rewards individuals based on loyalty to political interests rather than their qualifications or commitment to public service. To combat this, Patel calls for reforms that would prioritize merit-based hiring and promotion, ensuring that government employees are selected based on their ability to serve the public and their adherence to ethical standards.

Lastly, Patel believes that eliminating bureaucratic corruption requires a cultural shift in how government employees view their roles. Public service, in his view, should be about serving the American people and upholding the Constitution—not advancing one's personal interests or political ideology. By instilling this sense of duty and patriotism within government agencies, Patel believes that it is possible to restore the integrity of the federal government and eliminate the bureaucratic corruption that has so deeply undermined public trust.

In conclusion, Kash Patel's leadership philosophy in action revolves around building a team of American patriots who are committed to serving the public and restoring the nation's institutions. His approach to eliminating bureaucratic corruption focuses on transparency, accountability, and a commitment to hiring individuals who prioritize public service over political loyalty. By fostering a culture of integrity and ensuring that those in power are held to the highest ethical standards, Patel believes that it is possible to transform the government and put America back on the right track.

Chapter 6: Revolutionizing Federal Law Enforcement

Modernizing the FBI for the 21st Century

Kash Patel has long been a vocal critic of the FBI's structure, management, and direction, and his vision for the agency's future focuses on revolutionizing federal law enforcement to meet the evolving needs of modern society. In the ever-changing landscape of national security threats, from terrorism to cyberattacks, Patel recognizes that the FBI must adapt swiftly to new challenges. His approach emphasizes modernization and streamlining the FBI's operations, ensuring that the agency becomes more agile and responsive to emerging threats.

At the heart of Patel's vision is the idea of cutting down the bureaucratic layers that often slow down decision-making and hinder effectiveness. By creating a more dynamic, responsive structure, Patel believes the FBI can better tackle the pressing issues of our time. He has proposed restructuring the agency's top-down hierarchy, encouraging a focus on frontline agents who deal directly with national security concerns, rather than an overabundance of administrative layers that can cloud the agency's mission. Patel's concept of modernization involves the use of advanced technology to enhance investigations, ensuring that the FBI keeps up with global advancements in intelligence gathering and counterterrorism measures.

One of Patel's major concerns is that the FBI has become bogged down by an entrenched bureaucratic culture that sometimes fails to prioritize its primary mission: protecting Americans from external and internal threats. His vision includes harnessing the power of data analytics, artificial intelligence, and new surveillance technologies to bolster the FBI's intelligence-gathering capabilities. This would allow the agency to quickly identify and respond to threats, whether they stem from terrorist organizations, foreign adversaries, or domestic extremists. Additionally, Patel advocates for a larger emphasis on cyber threats, believing the FBI should work closely with other agencies to secure the digital infrastructure of the United States from hacking and cyber warfare.

To realize this transformation, Patel would need to implement sweeping reforms to the agency's training, recruitment, and technology strategies. Modernizing the FBI's technology and training methods, ensuring that agents are equipped with the skills needed to operate in a tech-driven world, would be essential. Patel would focus on ensuring that agents are trained to understand and combat cyber threats, which have increasingly become the primary focus of national security operations. This modernization initiative would also likely involve an overhaul of the FBI's operational procedures, with a greater emphasis on real-time intelligence sharing and collaboration with state and local law enforcement agencies to ensure a swift and unified response to any threat.

While some critics might fear that such a radical shift could undermine the agency's traditional role, Patel's response is clear: modernizing the FBI is necessary to protect American citizens in an era of rapidly evolving technology and diverse national security challenges. By enhancing the FBI's ability to adapt to these new realities, Patel envisions an agency that not only serves its core mission more effectively but also better supports the broader goals of national security and justice in the 21st century.

Focusing on National Security and Counterterrorism

Kash Patel's extensive background in national security and counterterrorism has played a crucial role in shaping his vision for the FBI's future. As a former terrorism prosecutor and a senior official on the National Security Council, Patel has a deep understanding of the threats facing the United States. For him, counterterrorism is not just about protecting the nation from the conventional threats posed by groups like ISIS or al-Qaeda; it's also about addressing the growing array of threats posed by hostile state actors, such as China and Russia, as well as domestic terror cells and cyber threats.

Patel advocates for a comprehensive approach to national security that includes strengthening counterterrorism capabilities and ensuring that the FBI is properly equipped to deal with both international and domestic terrorism. His experience in national security law and intelligence has shaped his view that the FBI must not only be reactive to terrorist threats but also proactive in identifying and dismantling terrorist networks before they can execute attacks. This means investing in better intelligence gathering, increasing cooperation between federal agencies, and making use of advanced technology to stay ahead of potential threats.

Under Patel's vision, the FBI would place an even greater emphasis on international cooperation with allied intelligence agencies. The world is more interconnected than ever, and international terrorism knows no borders.

Patel's approach includes a stronger focus on information-sharing with global law enforcement and intelligence agencies, ensuring that the FBI has access to the best intelligence from around the world to prevent attacks before they happen. His administration of the FBI would focus on expanding relationships with NATO partners, as well as intelligence agencies in the Middle East and Europe, to create a comprehensive global security network.

In the realm of domestic counterterrorism, Patel would push for more robust measures to combat the rise of homegrown extremists. From anti-government militias to violent ideologies that inspire lone-wolf attacks, domestic terrorism is an ever-growing concern. Patel's strategy to tackle this problem would involve strengthening the FBI's intelligence-gathering operations in the United States, focusing on social media, internet forums, and other online spaces where radicalization takes place. Patel is keenly aware of how extremist ideologies can take root in digital communities, and his vision for counterterrorism includes a more proactive approach to monitoring and dismantling radical groups within the United States.

Moreover, Patel advocates for a greater focus on combating cyberterrorism. In an age where hacking, cyber espionage, and digital terrorism are on the rise, he believes the FBI must evolve to address these new kinds of threats. This includes improving the agency's cyber capabilities and strengthening its ability to investigate and counter cyberattacks that may be state-sponsored or perpetrated by independent actors. Patel's vision for the FBI includes working more closely with private sector cybersecurity companies, helping to protect critical infrastructure and national security assets from digital breaches.

Patel's focus on national security and counterterrorism goes beyond just keeping the country safe; it's also about adapting to the changing nature of modern threats. Whether those threats come from foreign nations, domestic extremist groups, or cyberattacks, Patel believes that the FBI must be fully prepared and well-equipped to respond swiftly and decisively. His vision for the FBI is one of strength, agility, and modernized capabilities, ensuring that the agency remains a cornerstone of American security in the years to come.

Chapter 7: Justice for All – A Vision for the DOJ

Cleaning House: Overhauling Leadership at the Department of Justice

One of the cornerstones of Kash Patel's vision for America's future is the overhaul of the Department of Justice (DOJ). With a career spent deeply embedded in national security and legal reform, Patel believes that the DOJ, the agency tasked with ensuring fairness and upholding the rule of law, has become increasingly politicized and is no longer operating in a manner that serves the American people equitably. Under his leadership, Patel envisions a DOJ that is free from partisan influences, putting the interests of justice above all else.

The first step in Patel's vision for reform would be to clean house at the highest levels of the DOJ. He has argued that the leadership at the agency has become entrenched in a culture of favoritism, bias, and political maneuvering, compromising the integrity of the department. Patel has openly called for a review of senior DOJ officials, with an eye toward removing those who are perceived to have compromised the department's impartiality for political reasons. This is not an attack on individual career prosecutors or agents but rather a recognition that leadership is key in ensuring the department's mission remains focused on law and justice, not on party politics.

Patel's vision for overhauling leadership at the DOJ involves bringing in fresh faces who are committed to restoring the agency's independence and credibility. He believes that individuals who have spent too much time in the Washington political swamp have lost touch with the everyday concerns of Americans. To remedy this, Patel envisions a DOJ led by people who are not just qualified but who have also shown a commitment to fairness and transparency throughout their careers. These individuals would be tasked with breaking down the entrenched bureaucracy that often stymies progress and addressing any systematic issues that have allowed political influence to creep into the department's operations.

The notion of political interference in the justice system has become increasingly apparent in recent years, with allegations of partisanship tainting investigations, prosecutions, and high-profile legal decisions. Patel's response to these concerns is clear: the DOJ must be shielded from political pressures. His vision for a clean DOJ would see the agency return to its roots, where impartiality is the guiding principle, and where decisions are based solely on facts and evidence, not political agendas. As part of this, Patel would call for reforms that encourage more transparency in how decisions are made, especially in high-profile cases that have significant public interest.

Central to this clean-up effort would be an overhaul of the DOJ's hiring and promotion processes. Patel has spoken about the importance of selecting leaders who are driven by the values of justice and integrity, not by their political connections. This would mean ensuring that the people at the helm of the DOJ are held to the highest ethical standards and are capable of resisting external political pressures that could influence their work. Patel would ensure that hiring decisions are based on merit, not on political loyalty, creating an environment where professionalism, competence, and justice take precedence over political considerations.

Moreover, Patel would push for more aggressive monitoring and accountability systems within the DOJ, ensuring that any actions that could compromise its independence are swiftly addressed. This includes creating oversight mechanisms that would allow the public and lawmakers to hold the DOJ accountable, while also safeguarding against partisan attacks that could undermine its mission.

Creating a Truly Apolitical Federal Agency

A key theme in Patel's vision for the DOJ is the creation of a truly apolitical federal agency. He sees a nation where justice is not swayed by the whims of political tides but is instead driven by an unwavering commitment to fairness and the rule of law. This vision for an apolitical DOJ is rooted in the belief that the American people deserve a justice system that operates independently of the executive branch, Congress, and political parties. For Patel, the DOJ should be a body that is fully dedicated to justice and the protection of constitutional rights, not to advancing any political agenda.

The importance of an apolitical DOJ cannot be overstated. When the justice system is perceived as being politically motivated, it undermines public trust in its effectiveness and fairness. Patel recognizes that this perception has been growing in recent years, especially with highly contentious political investigations and prosecutions. In his eyes, the solution is to remove partisan influences from the DOJ entirely, so that the department can operate based on the rule of law, free from the pressure of political considerations.

To create this apolitical environment, Patel would advocate for structural changes that insulate the DOJ from partisan interference. One such reform would be to ensure that the Attorney General, as well as other key leadership positions within the DOJ, are appointed based on merit rather than political considerations. Patel has expressed his belief that appointments should prioritize qualifications and expertise in law, criminal justice, and public service over political allegiances. His vision for a truly apolitical DOJ would also involve strict guidelines and transparency for political appointees, to ensure that their actions are aligned with the agency's commitment to justice, rather than political convenience.

Patel's idea of an apolitical DOJ extends beyond leadership appointments. He proposes a system where DOJ decisions, especially those concerning high-profile investigations or prosecutions, are made based on strict legal principles and facts, not on political agendas or party lines. This means ensuring that career prosecutors, agents, and legal experts within the DOJ are able to pursue their cases without fear of political interference or retaliation. Under Patel's leadership, the DOJ would adopt a set of ethical guidelines that mandate impartiality in all legal matters, with mechanisms in place to detect and address any potential conflicts of interest that may arise.

In addition to protecting the DOJ from political influence, Patel also envisions a system where public confidence in the department is restored. He has stated that transparency is key to rebuilding trust, and he believes that the DOJ must operate in a way that is both visible and accountable to the American people. Under his proposed reforms, Patel would call for regular reporting on the DOJ's activities, including the status of high-profile cases, the rationale behind key legal decisions, and any steps the department is taking to ensure fairness and justice.

Moreover, Patel would push for reforms that allow for more collaboration and coordination between different federal agencies, while still maintaining the DOJ's independence. He believes that the department must work alongside other law enforcement and intelligence agencies in the fight against crime and terrorism, but that these collaborations should always be conducted within the bounds of the law and without political influence.

The ultimate goal of Patel's efforts would be to create a DOJ that is viewed by the public as fair, impartial, and above reproach. In his vision, the department would become a shining example of what a federal agency should be—dedicated to serving the American people by ensuring that justice is administered without bias or favoritism, and that the rule of law prevails regardless of political winds.

In conclusion, Kash Patel's vision for the DOJ is centered around cleaning up the agency's leadership, restoring its impartiality, and ensuring that it operates free from political influence. Through these reforms, Patel hopes to restore the public's faith in the justice system, ensuring that it works for all Americans, not just those in power. The DOJ, under Patel's leadership, would be a body that focuses on one thing above all: ensuring justice for every citizen, no matter their background or political affiliation.

Chapter 8: The Role of Media and Technology in Justice

Holding Big Tech Accountable for Election Integrity

In the digital age, the role of technology companies and social media platforms in shaping public opinion and influencing political outcomes cannot be overstated. Kash Patel is acutely aware of the growing power of Big Tech companies, particularly when it comes to their influence on election integrity. He believes that these companies have a moral and legal responsibility to ensure that their platforms are not used to undermine democratic processes.

Patel's vision for holding Big Tech accountable begins with a robust framework of regulations and oversight that prevents these companies from interfering in elections. His primary concern is the ability of tech giants to censor or manipulate information, often under the guise of combating "misinformation" or "hate speech." While these platforms have vast reach and the power to shape narratives, Patel believes their unchecked control over the flow of information poses a threat to the free exchange of ideas.

Under Patel's leadership, efforts would be made to establish clear guidelines on what constitutes election interference and to hold companies accountable for any role they play in undermining democratic processes. This includes preventing any form of bias or censorship that could favor one political ideology over another, particularly during election seasons. Patel would push for greater transparency from tech companies about how they moderate content and enforce policies, ensuring that they do not suppress voices based on political affiliation or personal beliefs.

Additionally, Patel envisions a federal commission dedicated to monitoring the activities of tech companies during election periods. This commission would have the authority to investigate and take action against any tech giant found to be violating election integrity standards. In Patel's view, companies that control the flow of information on a global scale must be held to the highest standards of accountability, ensuring they operate in a way that respects the democratic process and the rights of citizens to freely participate in elections.

Another critical aspect of Patel's vision for election integrity is the role of transparency in the algorithms used by social media platforms. Many platforms operate on algorithms that are opaque and highly secretive, making it difficult to determine how content is being promoted or suppressed. Patel calls for these algorithms to be made publicly available, so users and lawmakers can assess whether they are being manipulated to serve particular political agendas.

Patel's emphasis on transparency and accountability extends to the use of data by tech companies. Big Tech firms collect vast amounts of personal information, which they use to target users with specific political messaging. Patel is deeply concerned about how this data is used, often without the knowledge or consent of the individuals it's collected from. He would push for greater oversight over data usage, ensuring that personal information is not exploited to influence voters in a way that undermines the principles of free and fair elections.

Combatting Media Misinformation with Facts

The spread of misinformation, particularly through media channels and social media platforms, is another area where Kash Patel sees a need for significant reform. While he acknowledges the importance of a free press, Patel is concerned about the growing influence of media outlets that prioritize sensationalism and partisanship over factual reporting. The rise of "fake news" and biased reporting has eroded trust in the media, and Patel believes that restoring integrity to the media landscape is essential for the future of democracy.

One of the key components of Patel's plan to combat media misinformation is promoting journalistic standards that prioritize truth over agenda. He believes that media outlets must be held accountable for spreading false information and that there should be more stringent regulations in place to prevent the dissemination of misleading or inaccurate news. At the same time, Patel is wary of overregulation, as he firmly supports the First Amendment and the freedom of the press. His approach would strike a balance between protecting the free press and ensuring that media outlets are held to ethical standards.

To this end, Patel envisions the creation of an independent body to fact-check media claims, particularly when it comes to issues of national security, elections, and public health. This body would be tasked with verifying the accuracy of news stories and ensuring that any false or misleading information is swiftly corrected. The goal would not be to censor media outlets but to provide a counterbalance to the increasing spread of misinformation.

Patel is also a proponent of educating the public on how to critically assess media and information sources. He believes that an informed citizenry is the best defense against misinformation. This includes promoting media literacy programs that teach individuals how to identify credible sources, understand biases, and recognize propaganda. Patel argues that this educational approach, combined with accountability for media outlets, can help restore trust in the press and ensure that the public is not swayed by misinformation.

Additionally, Patel advocates for the creation of a legal framework that holds media outlets accountable for the harm caused by false information. While defamation laws already exist, Patel would like to see stronger measures in place for instances where media outlets deliberately spread falsehoods that damage reputations, incite violence, or disrupt democratic processes. By introducing more stringent penalties for media outlets that repeatedly engage in spreading misinformation, Patel believes that a culture of accountability can be cultivated, restoring trust in the media.

Patel's approach to combatting misinformation is rooted in the belief that the truth must always come to light, even in an age where information is often manipulated for political gain. His strategy combines regulatory oversight, education, and legal reform to create an environment where facts are valued, and media outlets are held accountable for their role in shaping public perception. Through these efforts, Patel aims to restore faith in the media and ensure that the information Americans rely on is truthful, balanced, and in service of the public good.

By tackling the issue of media misinformation and holding Big Tech accountable for its influence on election integrity, Patel envisions a society where facts take precedence over agendas, and the public can rely on a free, fair, and transparent information ecosystem. In the context of his broader vision for justice and reform, this approach is essential for protecting democracy and ensuring that all Americans have access to accurate information that empowers them to make informed decisions.

Chapter 9: Kash Patel's National Security Expertise

Lessons Learned from Counterterrorism Prosecution

Kash Patel's expertise in national security is built on his extensive experience working on some of the most significant counterterrorism prosecutions in U.S. history. Throughout his career, Patel has consistently emphasized the importance of understanding both the strategic and tactical elements of counterterrorism efforts. His insights into these areas come not only from his time as a federal prosecutor but also from his work in various national security roles, including as the Deputy Director for Counterterrorism at the National Security

Council and as the Chief of Staff at the Department of Defense.

One of Patel's key lessons from his time in counterterrorism prosecution is the critical need for coordination between various agencies within the U.S. government. In dealing with terrorism and national security threats, no single entity can effectively combat these issues on its own. Instead, it requires a united front from intelligence agencies, law enforcement, and the Department of Defense. This belief underpins Patel's approach to national security, which centers on fostering greater inter-agency cooperation to address threats more efficiently.

In his role as a prosecutor, Patel dealt with terrorist suspects who posed an immediate threat to American interests. His hands-on experience with these cases has provided him with a nuanced understanding of how to approach and dismantle terrorist networks. He learned that successful prosecutions are not just about capturing individuals but also about gathering the intelligence necessary to prevent future attacks. This insight has guided his thinking as he moves forward in his national security endeavors.

A key takeaway from Patel's counterterrorism work is the importance of keeping a long-term perspective when confronting such threats. He stresses that while immediate actions, such as arrests and prosecutions, are vital, the broader strategy of disrupting and dismantling terrorist organizations must be built over time. This requires ongoing intelligence collection, strategic military action, and working with international partners to understand the global networks that support terrorist groups. Patel's firsthand involvement in these efforts has shaped his philosophy on national security, which is based on both swift action and long-term planning.

Patel also learned valuable lessons in dealing with the legal and constitutional challenges that arise in counterterrorism cases. The balance between national security and civil liberties is a delicate one, and his experiences have shaped his approach to ensuring that security measures are both effective and respectful of the rights guaranteed by the Constitution. He has consistently advocated for policies that prioritize protecting American citizens while safeguarding their civil liberties, particularly in the context of surveillance, detention, and due process. These principles remain central to his vision for national security.

Finally, Patel's time prosecuting terrorism cases reinforced the importance of staying ahead of emerging threats. Terrorist organizations are constantly evolving, utilizing new tactics and technologies to circumvent traditional security measures. Patel has consistently emphasized the need for the U.S. to remain agile and proactive, continually adapting its national security strategies to address these evolving threats. This mindset drives much of his approach to national security and his advocacy for investing in new technologies, intelligence-gathering methods, and defense mechanisms to combat modern threats.

Bridging the Gap Between Intelligence and Law Enforcement

One of the central tenets of Kash Patel's national security vision is bridging the gap between intelligence agencies and law enforcement. Throughout his career, Patel has witnessed the often-fragmented relationship between these two critical components of the U.S. government's efforts to protect the country.

In Patel's view, the lack of coordination between these entities has hindered the nation's ability to respond swiftly and effectively to national security threats.

Patel is acutely aware that intelligence and law enforcement serve different, yet complementary, roles in safeguarding the nation. Intelligence agencies, such as the CIA and NSA, are tasked with gathering information about potential threats, often through covert means, while law enforcement agencies, like the FBI, are responsible for investigating and prosecuting crimes. However, these two branches have often operated in silos, resulting in missed opportunities for early intervention and a lack of comprehensive responses to national security challenges.

Kash Patel is committed to improving collaboration between intelligence agencies and law enforcement. He believes that fostering better communication and cooperation between these entities is essential for ensuring that intelligence is translated into actionable law enforcement responses. By breaking down the walls that separate these organizations, Patel envisions a system where information is shared more freely and swiftly, allowing both intelligence and law enforcement officials to act on threats in real-time.

To achieve this, Patel proposes the creation of integrated task forces that include members from both intelligence and law enforcement agencies. These task forces would focus on specific threats, such as terrorism or cyberattacks, and would be empowered to coordinate their efforts seamlessly. Patel believes that this type of collaboration is critical for identifying and neutralizing threats before they escalate into full-blown attacks.

One of the most significant obstacles to effective coordination between intelligence and law enforcement is the legal framework that governs how information is shared. National security laws, particularly those related to surveillance and wiretapping, have long been a source of tension between the intelligence community and law enforcement. Patel understands the importance of ensuring that intelligence agencies have the legal tools they need to monitor potential threats, but he also advocates for safeguards to protect individual privacy and civil liberties.

Under Patel's leadership, efforts would be made to reform and streamline the legal framework that governs intelligence-sharing. He advocates for reforms to the Foreign Intelligence Surveillance Act (FISA) to allow greater flexibility in how intelligence agencies share information with law enforcement, while still adhering to constitutional protections. Patel believes that this reform is necessary to ensure that law enforcement can act quickly when presented with critical intelligence, without the delays that often occur due to legal hurdles.

Patel's efforts to bridge the gap between intelligence and law enforcement also extend to the use of technology. He envisions investing in new technologies that will facilitate real-time data sharing and analysis between these agencies. By utilizing advanced tools for data analysis, encryption, and secure communication, Patel believes that the U.S. can create a more responsive and interconnected national security system.

Another key aspect of Patel's vision is enhancing collaboration between U.S. agencies and their international counterparts. National security threats are often global in nature, and Patel believes that the U.S. must work closely with allies and partners to share intelligence and coordinate law enforcement actions. Strengthening international relationships is a critical component of Patel's broader strategy for keeping the U.S. safe from emerging threats.

In conclusion, Patel's approach to bridging the gap between intelligence and law enforcement is rooted in the belief that effective national security requires a unified, coordinated response. By fostering better communication, streamlining legal frameworks, and investing in advanced technologies, Patel envisions a more agile and responsive security system that can swiftly address the evolving challenges of modern-day threats. His efforts to break down silos and integrate intelligence and law enforcement agencies are central to his vision of a safer, more secure America.

Chapter 10: Inspiring the Next Generation of Leaders

Empowering Veterans and Active Service Members Through Foundations

Kash Patel's commitment to national security extends beyond the halls of government and into the broader community, particularly when it comes to empowering veterans and active service members. Throughout his career, Patel has demonstrated a profound respect for those who have served in the military, understanding that they are the bedrock upon which America's freedom and security are built. One of Patel's core beliefs is that the country must do more to support those who have dedicated their lives to defending the nation.

In this chapter, Patel outlines his vision for empowering veterans and active service members through various foundations, initiatives, and programs that focus on providing both immediate and long-term support. He advocates for greater access to resources, such as healthcare, mental health services, education, and career development, to ensure that veterans and active-duty military personnel are equipped for success both during and after their service.

Patel is particularly passionate about helping veterans transition back into civilian life, recognizing that the challenges they face can be immense. The shift from military to civilian life is not always a smooth one, and many veterans encounter difficulties in finding employment, obtaining proper healthcare, and reintegrating into their communities. To address these challenges, Patel supports the establishment of foundations and organizations that are specifically designed to assist veterans in their transitions.

Patel envisions a system where veterans can have access to mentoring programs, job placement services, and educational opportunities that allow them to thrive in civilian careers. He believes that veterans have a wealth of experience, discipline, and leadership skills that can be harnessed to serve the country in new ways. By facilitating their transition to civilian life and empowering them to pursue new endeavors, Patel aims to ensure that veterans remain integral to the country's success, both economically and socially.

One of Patel's key initiatives would be creating partnerships between government agencies, private industry, and nonprofit organizations to build a comprehensive network of support for veterans and service members. This network would include resources for mental health, career advancement, and social reintegration, as well as opportunities to engage with other veterans in leadership roles. Patel has seen firsthand the powerful leadership potential within the military community, and he believes that tapping into this potential can help strengthen the nation.

Patel is also keenly aware of the need to support active service members while they are still in uniform. He advocates for initiatives that prioritize the well-being of soldiers and military families, particularly when it comes to reducing the stress and strain caused by extended deployments. By investing in the health, welfare, and education of service members, Patel believes that the military will remain a strong, resilient force that can effectively protect American interests around the world.

Education and Mentorship as Keys to National Strength

In addition to his work with veterans and active service members, Kash Patel strongly believes in the power of education and mentorship as foundational elements of national strength. The ability to lead, serve, and protect the nation starts with the development of young people who are equipped with the right values, skills, and knowledge. Patel's educational philosophy centers on creating opportunities for the next generation to learn from experienced leaders and mentors, fostering a culture of service, patriotism, and leadership that will continue to shape the future of America.

Patel understands that the nation's strength lies in its ability to cultivate and nurture the next generation of leaders. In order to achieve this, he advocates for a comprehensive approach to education that emphasizes critical thinking, a strong understanding of American history and values, and the development of leadership skills. He believes that the country must invest in education at all levels—from primary school to higher education—to ensure that young people are prepared to take on the challenges of the future.

One of the key components of Patel's vision is mentorship. He believes that young people need guidance and support from experienced leaders who can help them navigate the complexities of the modern world. By establishing mentorship programs that connect young individuals with seasoned professionals in fields such as law, politics, business, and the military, Patel hopes to create a pipeline of leaders who are well-prepared to take on important roles in society.

Patel has witnessed firsthand the profound impact that mentorship can have on an individual's personal and professional development. Many of the lessons he learned throughout his own career came from mentors who provided guidance, wisdom, and a sense of purpose. He believes that mentoring the next generation of leaders is one of the most important responsibilities of those who have had success in their fields.

To implement this vision, Patel has advocated for mentorship programs within schools, colleges, and professional organizations. These programs would match young people with mentors who can offer advice, share experiences, and help guide their career paths. By fostering relationships between mentees and mentors, Patel believes that young people will gain the confidence and skills needed to succeed in their chosen fields.

Education and mentorship go hand in hand in Patel's approach to national strength. He sees education as the foundation upon which leadership is built, while mentorship provides the guidance necessary to turn potential into action. In Patel's vision, every young person—regardless of their background—would have the opportunity to receive quality education and be mentored by individuals who have a vested interest in their success.

Patel is also focused on creating educational opportunities that will prepare the next generation for service to the country. Whether through military service, public service, or business ventures, Patel believes that every young person can contribute to the nation's future. As such, he is a strong advocate for expanding access to programs that foster leadership skills and provide the tools necessary for success in service-oriented careers.

In conclusion, Kash Patel's focus on empowering veterans and active service members, along with his commitment to education and mentorship, represents a comprehensive approach to strengthening the nation. By providing support to those who have served in the military and equipping the next generation with the tools they need to lead, Patel is working to ensure that the U.S. remains a strong, resilient, and forward-looking nation. The work of empowering individuals, whether through education, mentorship, or advocacy, is foundational to Patel's vision for the future of America.

Chapter 11: The Kash Patel Doctrine

Merging Policy and Action for True Justice Reform

The *Kash Patel Doctrine* represents a strategic framework for achieving lasting justice reform in the United States. Unlike many abstract or theoretical policy approaches, Patel's doctrine seeks to merge concrete action with policy, ensuring that reforms not only look good on paper but also translate into meaningful, real-world change. Through his career in national security, law enforcement, and government, Patel has consistently championed principles that focus on accountability, efficiency, and integrity as the bedrock of any meaningful justice system.

The need for reform in the justice system has never been more pressing, as issues such as corruption, political influence, and inefficiencies persist across federal agencies, including the FBI, DOJ, and other branches of law enforcement. Patel's doctrine emphasizes that true justice reform can only be achieved through a fundamental restructuring that addresses these systemic issues at their core. It's not merely about changing laws or issuing executive orders; it's about fostering a culture of transparency and a commitment to law and order that transcends political influence.

The essence of the Kash Patel Doctrine lies in its insistence on accountability and action. For Patel, the implementation of policy reforms must involve the active engagement of leadership and personnel, as well as the necessary structural changes to ensure the system's integrity. A passive policy approach, he argues, is insufficient to combat the entrenched problems in federal law enforcement and national security institutions. The changes must be both comprehensive and deeply rooted in the principles of fairness, justice, and national security.

The doctrine outlines a multi-tiered approach to reform. It begins with a commitment to enforcing existing laws more effectively, ensuring that justice is delivered consistently across all cases, regardless of political influence or public opinion. From this foundation, Patel advocates for reforms that will modernize agencies like the FBI and DOJ, reduce bureaucratic red tape, and cut out corruption at every level. Additionally, the *Kash Patel Doctrine* encourages a transparent system where the American public can have faith that justice is being served with equal rigor, from law enforcement officers to high-ranking political officials.

Principles of Accountability, Efficiency, and Integrity

The core principles of accountability, efficiency, and integrity are central to the Kash Patel Doctrine and serve as the guiding principles in his approach to justice reform. Each principle plays a pivotal role in Patel's vision of a reformed, effective justice system. These principles not only define the framework for reform but also serve as the standard by which all future actions and policies are judged.

1. Accountability: A Commitment to Transparency and Responsibility

Accountability is perhaps the most critical element of the Kash Patel Doctrine. Without accountability, the justice system risks becoming a tool for political leverage or corruption, rendering it ineffective and unjust. Patel emphasizes that accountability must be the foundation of any reform effort, requiring both individual responsibility and institutional transparency.

The first aspect of accountability, Patel argues, is ensuring that leaders at the highest levels of the Department of Justice, FBI, and other federal agencies are held to rigorous standards. This includes creating an environment where leadership can be scrutinized and held accountable for their decisions. A key facet of accountability, according to Patel, is ending the culture of impunity that exists for high-ranking officials. Whether it's in the case of mishandling classified information, abuse of power, or any illegal actions, Patel insists that those in positions of authority should face consequences just as much as ordinary citizens.

Furthermore, Patel stresses the need for a transparent oversight system. A robust system of checks and balances must be in place, one that provides the public with insight into how decisions are being made and how those decisions impact the nation. Transparency is not only vital for restoring trust in institutions but also essential for preventing misuse of power and authority. Patel proposes independent oversight bodies, such as citizen review boards, to hold agencies accountable for their actions.

2. Efficiency: Streamlining the Justice System

The principle of efficiency focuses on reforming the processes and structures of the justice system so that it can more effectively deliver justice in a timely manner. Patel argues that the current system is bogged down by bureaucracy, excessive paperwork, and outdated procedures that slow down investigations and legal proceedings. This inefficiency, he contends, is a major obstacle to achieving justice in a timely fashion.

The inefficiencies within the justice system not only frustrate the American public but also embolden criminals and corrupt actors who exploit these delays. Patel's vision includes streamlining agency operations and implementing new technologies to improve the speed and accuracy of investigations. For example, modernizing record-keeping systems, improving data management techniques, and enhancing information-sharing between agencies are all part of Patel's plan to create a faster, more responsive justice system.

Patel's focus on efficiency also extends to eliminating unnecessary government intervention and reducing redundancies between agencies. By creating a more agile and coordinated approach between law enforcement and intelligence agencies, Patel envisions a justice system that is better equipped to tackle modern challenges, such as cyber threats, domestic terrorism, and organized crime. Efficiency does not mean rushing to conclusions or cutting corners, Patel stresses, but rather ensuring that the system works smoothly and effectively without unnecessary obstacles.

3. Integrity: Upholding the Rule of Law Above All Else

Integrity is the cornerstone of the Kash Patel Doctrine. Patel stresses that in order to restore faith in the justice system, officials must act with the highest levels of integrity. This means adhering to the rule of law, maintaining ethical standards, and putting the interests of justice above personal or political gain.

The principle of integrity requires a commitment to serving the American public with honesty and fairness, regardless of political pressure or special interests. Patel believes that the justice system has been compromised by partisan politics and that it is essential to return to a place where decisions are based solely on the merits of the case and not influenced by political affiliations or personal ambitions.

A major aspect of upholding integrity is creating a culture of honor and professionalism within law enforcement agencies. Patel advocates for ensuring that those who serve in federal law enforcement and intelligence agencies understand their sacred duty to protect and serve the American people. This involves instilling a deep respect for the Constitution and the principles upon which the nation was founded.

The integrity principle also extends to ensuring that all individuals, regardless of race, gender, or background, are treated equally under the law. Patel's vision for justice reform includes dismantling any discriminatory practices and ensuring that the justice system works impartially for all Americans.

In summary, the *Kash Patel Doctrine* represents a comprehensive, actionable blueprint for transforming the justice system into an institution that works efficiently, transparently, and with unwavering integrity. By focusing on accountability, efficiency, and integrity, Patel offers a vision that seeks not only to reform existing institutions but to restore trust in the government and the justice system as a whole. The future of American justice, as Patel envisions it, is one where the rule of law prevails above all, where the government serves the people, and where the principles of fairness and equality are upheld in every corner of the justice system.

Chapter 12: Looking to the Future

Envisioning a Justice System Free of Bias

As the nation looks toward the future, one of the key goals for reforming the American justice system is to create an environment where justice is truly blind — a system free of bias and political influence. For Kash Patel, this vision is central to his enduring legacy and is a focal point of his long-term strategy for national security, law enforcement, and judicial reform.

Patel has been a vocal critic of the entrenched biases he believes plague the justice system, particularly within agencies like the FBI and the Department of Justice (DOJ). His argument rests on the notion that when the system allows biases to influence decisions, whether based on political party, race, or personal interests, it undermines public trust and renders the justice process unfair and inequitable. He stresses that a justice system rooted in bias cannot deliver justice for all, especially when some individuals or groups are treated differently from others due to external factors.

In his vision for the future, Patel advocates for the creation of a truly impartial system — one where decisions are based purely on facts, evidence, and the rule of law. His proposal is not to remove subjective judgment from the system altogether but to ensure that judgment is exercised with fairness, transparency, and accountability. This requires a shift in the culture of federal agencies and law enforcement departments, with leadership committed to upholding the highest standards of integrity, objectivity, and equal treatment under the law.

Key to achieving this vision is reforming how federal agencies engage with the public, how they conduct investigations, and how they make legal decisions. Patel envisions an open system where scrutiny is not only welcome but encouraged. A system where all individuals, regardless of their status or political power, are held to the same standards and treated equally in the eyes of the law.

To realize this future, Patel advocates for:

1. **Bias Awareness and Sensitivity Training** – Making a concerted effort to train law enforcement and judicial personnel in identifying and addressing bias, whether implicit or explicit, within their work. This includes reevaluating hiring practices to ensure diversity and inclusion within leadership positions and throughout the ranks.

2. **Public Accountability Mechanisms** – Patel believes that the general public should be able to hold the justice system accountable. He has suggested mechanisms for transparent audits and regular reviews of government investigations, where external observers can identify and mitigate any biases in procedures or outcomes.

3. **Reform of Sentencing Guidelines** – By reducing mandatory minimum sentences and addressing disparities in how certain populations are treated by the justice system, Patel believes we can begin to chip away at longstanding racial and socio-economic biases.

Ultimately, the vision is one where every American has equal access to justice, and where the courts operate without prejudice, ensuring fair trials and impartial rulings. This ideal future, where bias is minimized and integrity upheld, is an essential part of Patel's legacy, as he firmly believes that only a fair system can truly serve the people of the United States.

Kash Patel's Legacy: Redefining Leadership in America

As a public servant, national security expert, and law enforcement reform advocate, Kash Patel has played an instrumental role in shaping the discourse on justice reform, national security, and government accountability. His legacy, however, is not defined simply by the positions he has held, but by his unwavering commitment to the values of transparency, fairness, and efficiency. Patel has continuously proven that leadership is not just about being in charge — it's about using influence to effect positive, lasting change in the public good.

One of Patel's core beliefs is that true leadership is measured not by titles or accolades but by the tangible, positive impact one has on the nation's institutions. Throughout his career, he has sought to redefine what it means to be a leader in America. For him, leadership is about courage — the courage to challenge the status quo, confront corruption, and advocate for reforms that benefit the American people, not political elites or special interests. Patel's leadership philosophy emphasizes moral clarity, decisiveness, and a willingness to confront uncomfortable truths, even when doing so might put him at odds with powerful institutions.

Patel's legacy also includes a steadfast commitment to the principles of the American Constitution. Throughout his career, he has emphasized that upholding constitutional values is the bedrock of any democratic system, and it is these values that must guide government actions. In Patel's view, leadership in America is about protecting the rights and freedoms of individuals, safeguarding the integrity of the rule of law, and defending the principles upon which the nation was founded.

As he looks to the future, Patel remains determined to instill these values in the next generation of leaders. His efforts to mentor young professionals in law, government, and national security have set the stage for a new wave of leadership that will prioritize these core principles in every aspect of public service. By focusing on integrity and efficiency in government, Patel has inspired a model of leadership that seeks to empower individuals to effect change for the betterment of all Americans.

Through his reforms in the FBI, DOJ, and the broader law enforcement community, Patel has left a legacy of structural change that will continue to shape the justice system for years to come. His push for greater transparency, fairness, and impartiality has paved the way for future reforms that will strive to ensure that all Americans are treated equally under the law, regardless of their political affiliations or social standing.

Moreover, Patel's impact extends beyond law enforcement. As a thought leader on national security, Patel has reshaped the discourse on how America approaches both domestic and international threats. His work in counterterrorism and intelligence has earned him respect from both sides of the political aisle, marking him as a key figure in the ongoing battle to secure America's safety without compromising its fundamental democratic principles.

Looking ahead, the ripple effects of Patel's leadership are expected to be felt across various sectors of American government. His commitment to fostering transparency, accountability, and constitutional fidelity will continue to inform policy and leadership decisions at the highest levels. Whether in law enforcement, national security, or public policy, Patel's example will inspire future leaders to act with integrity and to prioritize the public good over personal or partisan interests.

Ultimately, the Kash Patel legacy is one of principled leadership, relentless dedication to justice reform, and a vision of a more fair and transparent America. His efforts to rid the justice system of bias, combat corruption, and restore faith in public institutions will continue to influence the course of American history, leaving behind a framework for leaders to follow as they navigate the complexities of governing in the 21st century.

Patel's legacy is one of both action and vision — a legacy that reflects his commitment to a brighter future where justice is impartial, leadership is defined by integrity, and the rule of law stands as the bedrock of American democracy. As the next generation of leaders takes the mantle, Patel's influence will undoubtedly remain a guiding force in shaping the future of America's justice system and national security policies.

Conclusion

Kash Patel's Impact on America's Justice System

Kash Patel's influence on America's justice system is not simply confined to his actions in office or his tenure as a key figure in national security and law enforcement reform. His legacy is intertwined with the substantial changes he pushed for, the reforms he advocated, and the vision of a more transparent, accountable, and just system for all Americans.

Patel's impact began with a sharp critique of the status quo — particularly the entrenched corruption, bias, and inefficiency within the FBI, Department of Justice, and other critical elements of the justice apparatus. His critiques were not vague or superficial; they were grounded in a deep understanding of institutional dysfunction and a commitment to rectify the power imbalances that have long been woven into the fabric of American law enforcement and intelligence operations. From advocating for the decentralization of power within the FBI to exposing the inner workings of the "deep state," Patel has made it his mission to remove political influence from these vital sectors, ensuring that decisions are made on the basis of facts, not partisan motivations.

His leadership and determination have undeniably influenced the course of American law enforcement policy, shifting the conversation about accountability, transparency, and public trust. Patel has shown that national security and the protection of the American people must always be pursued with a sense of duty, honor, and integrity — not as a tool for political manipulation or control.

Under Patel's guidance, reforms aimed at protecting the rights of all citizens, irrespective of political or social status, gained momentum. His vision for a justice system that treats everyone equally and fairly has become a focal point for future leaders and policymakers. His willingness to challenge the system, regardless of political affiliation, helped bring attention to issues that were often swept under the rug. Through his work, he has started a movement within government and law enforcement to rethink how justice is administered, aiming to make it both impartial and efficient.

Patel's comprehensive approach to justice reform, including his recommendations for better law enforcement practices, restructuring the FBI, and eliminating partisan bias, has had a profound effect on how the American public perceives its justice system. His lasting influence will be felt for years to come, as future generations of leaders continue to build on the foundation he has laid.

A Vision Realized

Kash Patel's vision for justice reform has already started to take shape and, in many ways, has already been realized through the various steps he has taken to address issues within the FBI, DOJ, and other institutions. His leadership has sparked a broader movement focused on transparency, accountability, and restoring the public's trust in federal institutions. By championing policies that reduce bias, eliminate corruption, and put the interests of ordinary citizens at the forefront of government, Patel has demonstrated what it means to be a leader in the modern age — someone who prioritizes results over rhetoric, substance over symbolism.

Though his journey is far from over, the path that Patel has blazed is one that others will follow, adapting his principles to their own work and experiences. His work has been instrumental in exposing the entrenched challenges within the justice system, and his proposed reforms have helped set the stage for lasting change. His dedication to a future where justice is not only served but is perceived as fair and equitable by all Americans is at the heart of his legacy.

For Patel, true leadership is defined by the ability to bring about systemic change and to inspire others to adopt those reforms. His relentless pursuit of a fairer, more efficient justice system has brought significant attention to issues that affect not just law enforcement, but also national security, civil rights, and the broader health of American democracy.

As the country continues to wrestle with questions about the role of government, accountability, and transparency, Patel's influence will undoubtedly persist. His contributions have provided a new model for leadership that demands efficiency, ethics, and an unwavering commitment to the American people. His legacy is not merely that of a government official or reformer, but that of a visionary who had the courage to challenge conventional wisdom and advocate for a justice system that reflects the nation's highest ideals.

Patel's reforms, leadership philosophy, and long-term vision for the justice system will continue to inform the debates around law enforcement and national security for years to come. His imprint on the American justice system is already a critical part of the national conversation — a conversation that will continue to evolve, driven by the principles he has championed and the change he has inspired.

In the end, Kash Patel's legacy is one of profound impact — a legacy that has reshaped the landscape of American justice and will continue to influence generations of leaders who seek to build a more just and transparent future for all citizens. His vision has not only reshaped the institutions he has touched but has also inspired a new era of leadership, one that is focused on accountability, fairness, and the unwavering pursuit of justice for all.

Made in United States
Orlando, FL
11 April 2025

60378241R00075